A FOUR-WEEK
GUIDED EXPERIENCE FOR
INDIVIDUALS AND GROUPS

YOU ARE BLESSED, BLESSED... BLESSED

MISSY ROBERTSON

with *Ashley Wiersma*

**TYNDALE®
MOMENTUM**

An Imprint of Tyndale House Publishers, Inc.

Visit Tyndale online at www.tyndale.com.

Visit Tyndale Momentum online at www.tyndalemomentum.com.

Tyndale Momentum and the Tyndale Momentum logo are registered trademarks of Tyndale House Publishers, Inc. Tyndale Momentum is an imprint of Tyndale House Publishers, Inc., Carol Stream, Illinois.

Duck Commander is a trademark of Duck Commander, Inc. The *A&E* and *Duck Commander* logos are copyrighted and all rights reserved. Used with permission.

You Are Blessed, Blessed . . . Blessed: A Four-Week Guided Experience for Individuals and Groups

Copyright © 2015 by Missy Robertson. All rights reserved.

Cover photograph by Stephen Vosloo. Copyright © by Tyndale House Publishers, Inc. All rights reserved.

Cover photograph of wooden sign copyright © inxti/Shutterstock. All rights reserved.

Back cover images are the property of their respective copyright holders, and all rights are reserved. Mother duck copyright © Ewais/Shutterstock; ducklings copyright © nikolay100/Dollar Photo Club.

Interior images are the property of their respective copyright holders, and all rights are reserved. Heart puzzle and watercolor lettering by Caroline Hutchison. Copyright © by Tyndale House Publishers; banner copyright © creadib/Dollar Photo Club; frame copyright © Magdalena Kucova/Dollar Photo Club; lightbulb copyright © djvstock/Dollar Photo Club; ornaments copyright © Giraphics/Dollar Photo Club; boot © Tristan Tan/Shutterstock.

Photograph of Missy and Mia on necklace packaging taken by Steven Palowsky.

Designed by Ron Kaufmann

ISBN 978-1-4964-0571-5

Printed in the United States of America

21	20	19	18	17	16	15
7	6	5	4	3	2	

Table of Contents

A Note from Missy

~

Blessed, blessed . . . blessed. Many times, blessings are easy to spot: loving parents, a new baby, a great job. But sometimes blessings show up clothed in situations and challenges we didn't expect and definitely wouldn't have chosen for ourselves. A blessing like this typically peeks around the corner of our lives right when we're just rocking along, thinking everything is going pretty well. All of a sudden, *wham*! It hits us right between the eyes, and it in no way resembles anything "blessed." Based on Jase's and my personal experience, I've learned that it takes some time to recognize the blessings behind the burdens we bear. In fact, it can even take *years* of full-on commitment to peeling away layer after layer of hardship and sadness before we get to that blessing hidden way down deep.

Through all of our trials in life—especially a major one with our daughter, Mia, which is the central subject of this guided experience you hold—my husband and I have tried not only to stay the course of continually peeling off those layers together, but also to do our best to become better people—better parents, better spouses to each other, better friends to the people in our lives, and better children of God. We've tried to do more than survive our challenges; we've also endeavored to *thrive*. This is my hope for you, too.

The truth is that when something tragic happens in your life, you can choose to deny it, ignore it, and hope it gets better on its own, *or* you can choose to face it head-on and, under the tender care of a loving God, flourish in spite of the pain. A long time ago, I chose the latter. Jase and I both did. We were determined to deal with the difficulties and emerge *more* stable, *more* faithful, *more* loving, and *more* filled with peace on the other side. I chose to face the tragedy head-on for the simple reason that I believed God had created me for a purpose and had my best interest at heart. "If God is for us," Romans 8:31 plainly says, "who can ever be against us?" Things looked tragic, but I knew God was on my side. I knew there was purpose in the pain, and so I decided to work to discover what that purpose was.

I grew up in a preacher's home, the daughter of a very enthusiastic evangelist—someone whose job it was to tell anyone and everyone about the love of God and about the grace available to them because of the completed work of Jesus Christ. My dad spent his days explaining the gospel of Jesus—the "Good News," the Bible calls it—that in Christ we can be free of the things that weigh us down. We can live with an inner sense of being settled, of being completely and totally at peace. I had no idea as a child how invaluable those gifts would be to me later in life. How could I have known that decades later, after I'd gotten married and had three children, my world would be completely rocked by my sweet girl's physical challenges? Well, I may not have known, but God did. And to this day, I am humbled by the fact that He invited me into a relationship with Him all those years ago, knowing full well that that relationship would be my lifeline during some stormy weather that would soon be brewing on the horizon of my life.

What He knew that I couldn't yet understand was that I would never be able to experience those realities we all want in life—contentment, gratitude, steadiness, a deep-seated sense of rightness, all of the fruit of the Spirit that Galatians 5:22-23 describes—until I devoted myself to Him. After all, He invented all those things. Looking for peace and joy and happiness apart from God is about as ludicrous as going fishing in the desert; both end in futility every time.

Like me, you may be enjoying wonderful intimacy with Christ these days because at one point along the way, you realized that God wanted to relate with you and that He had already provided a means for connecting through the sacrifice of His Son, Jesus, on the cross. You surrendered your life to Him, told Him you wanted to go His way instead of your own, and began walking the path of righteousness, seeking His will above all else. But I recognize that for a certain percentage of the wonderful people who pick up this guide and begin working through its content, you aren't in *any* form of relationship with God right now, let alone a relationship you'd describe as intimate. If I'm talking about you here, then please know that I understand what it's like to have more questions than answers about God. I remember being a young woman who was filled to overflowing with curiosity about Him. Who is He? What does He want? What is it like to be in relationship with Someone you cannot see? Does relating with Him really make a difference in life at all?

Regardless of where you find yourself along the spiritual continuum—either deeply in love with Jesus or else deeply curious (or even skeptical) about Him—*you are welcome here*. This guided experience was created with the heartfelt desire for you to find a way through your pain, through your doubt, through your depression or sorrow or rage, and that you will persevere until you reach the blessing waiting for you at the other side. The tunnel may be very dark, but I assure you, the light will come. There, you will find peace. And it is my firm belief that there *you will find God*. He's waiting to help you in the same way He stood ready to help me all those years ago. And His message to us all—you and me and everyone else who suffers and struggles in this life—is that in Him, we are richly blessed.

At the end of this guide, you will have an opportunity to explore what beginning a personal relationship with God through His Son, Jesus Christ, looks like. I remain eternally grateful for my dear dad, who patiently walked me through the very same tenets of our faith that I will walk you through starting on page 97. There is no greater honor for me than to be the bearer of the *ultimate* good news in a person's life. If you choose to be "born again," as we'll discuss in the postscript, I hope you'll let me know by tweeting me at #blessedblessedblessed.

BlesSINGs, *
Missy Robertson
May 2015

*I always sign my name this way, emphasizing the word within the word because I love to sing—something I have been doing my entire life.

Before You Begin

~

Welcome to *You Are Blessed, Blessed . . . Blessed: A Four-Week Guided Experience for Individuals and Groups.* As Missy mentioned, it is her deep desire that you would experience the same level of peace and provision—fully and completely—that she and Jase have known as they've walked through the most tumultuous times in their lives. To that end, she and I (Ashley) have put together this guide aimed at helping you name the heaviest burden you're carrying these days and then navigate the path toward peace. Ready to dive in?

What You'll Need

To get the most out of *You Are Blessed, Blessed . . . Blessed,* have the following materials at hand each time you sit down to work through one of the parts:

→ *A copy of Missy's book* Blessed, Blessed . . . Blessed
→ *Your favorite Bible (This guide uses the New Living Translation, but any translation is fine.)*

> ✦ *Extra paper or a journal, in case you need more space to log your thoughts*
> ✦ *A pen*

How to Get Started

As you dig into each part of this guide, you'll notice a word of encouragement to read a few chapters of Missy's book. Doing so will ensure you're up to speed on the themes and stories referred to in each part, all of which come from the suggested reading. The schedule is as follows:

BEFORE BEGINNING . . .	BE SURE TO READ IN MISSY'S BOOK . . .
Part I: Name Your Burden	The introduction and chapters 1-3
Part II: Tell Your Truth	Chapters 4-6
Part III: Grow as You Go	Chapters 7-9
Part IV: Say Yes to "Blessed"	Chapters 10-12

Consider rallying a few friends, family members, or colleagues to walk through this experience with you. Certainly, you can work through the content on your own, but the best growth happens in community. While sharing your burdens aloud in the presence of other living, breathing human beings can feel a little scary at first, the support and strength you'll gain as a result of sojourning with others who also are choosing candor will be worth it in the end.

Once you confirm who will be joining you for the journey, choose a time and date to kick things off, and decide how frequently you will meet. This guide has been arranged according to four weeks' worth of content, but feel free to adjust that rhythm based on your group's specific needs.

Prior to your first meeting, ask every group member to complete all of part 1. This way, each participant will be prepared for the questions she or he will be asked to answer. Along these lines, throughout this guide you will notice "With Your Group" callouts; these questions make for fantastic road signs to lead your group through each part.

A quick note regarding facilitation: Depending on the composition of your group, you will want either to designate a facilitator who will lead all of the four group meetings, or to rotate those responsibilities week by week so that four individuals have the chance to lead.

What to Expect as You Go

This guide was designed to afford you lots of "processing" space, so take advantage of the journaling prompts, margins, and lined spaces for recording thoughts and ideas, knowing that all your jots and doodles will help you mark your progress as you go. Also, digging through the layer upon layer of pain that is always inherent in the burdens we bear can be quite an emotional experience. *Have grace toward yourself as you go.* Take your time. Ask God for help. And trust that your labor will not be in vain. (1 Corinthians 15:58)

If Missy's journey thus far declares anything, it is that despite life's most challenging circumstances, we can do more than get by; we can *thrive*. Fellow burden bearer, let the thriving begin.

PART I

Name Your Burden

TO PREPARE FOR PART I,

PLEASE READ THE INTRODUCTION AND CHAPTERS 1, 2, AND 3

IN MISSY'S BOOK BLESSED, BLESSED . . . BLESSED.

Here on earth you will have many trials and sorrows. But take heart, because I have overcome the world.

JESUS OF NAZARETH[1]

Many people would agree that the deepest need we human beings have is for control. Or at least a *sense* of control. We want to believe that we have a say in how our lives are going to turn out, that our opinions actually count regarding the circumstances we're willing to face.

This is why it is so upsetting to us when we learn that we have a horrible illness, or that the money that was supposed to come in isn't coming, or that the spouse we adore has had an affair. "This isn't what I signed up for," we silently protest. "This isn't how my life was supposed to turn out."

In chapter 1 of *Blessed, Blessed . . . Blessed*, Missy writes of two unexpected situations that would radically affect every single aspect of her life. One was the visibility that came from being part of the television show *Duck Dynasty*. The other, not nearly as joyous, was the realization that the perfect little girl she'd always dreamed of having would be born with special needs.

My Impossible Burden

As you come to this guided journal, you likely have a series of situations in your life that have unfolded in unexpected ways. You are in a different job than you thought you'd be in. Or you are living in a city you never thought you'd call home. Or a child of yours is making unwise decisions. Or your physical health has taken an unfortunate turn. Whatever the specific circumstance, perhaps it seems as if God has abandoned you to it, and the burden you now face seems impossible for you to bear.

What is the burden in your life you most wish God would lift? Write it on the following lines using as many, or as few, words as you'd like.

My Impossible Burden

_____

_____

_____

_____

Some "Impossible Burdens" We May Bear:
- *An ungrateful spouse*
- *An infertile womb*
- *Job loss and financial chaos*
- *The betrayal of a friend*
- *A wayward child*
- *A perplexing medical diagnosis*

WITH YOUR GROUP

If you're comfortable doing so, share with your group the burden you're bearing.

For most of us, our "impossible burden" is intensely upsetting because it represents an expectation we had for our lives that, to our great disappointment, is going unmet. We expect to have gainful employment, financial stability, a loving spouse, respectful children, and good health as we journey through this thing called life. We expect our family members to be supportive of us and our friends to be faithful to us. This is why it hurts deeply when our realities are not fulfilled.

With your impossible burden fresh on your mind, spend a few minutes thinking about the unmet expectations it represents. As it relates to the burden you are bearing, what goals or ideals did you have for your life that just aren't panning out? Log your thoughts on the following lines. An example has been provided for you.

Example: My *expectation* was that <u>I'd have a job by now</u>, but my *reality* is <u>still no work, still no hope</u>.

_____

_____

_____

_____

_____

_____

⊹ **WITH YOUR GROUP** ⊹

Discuss one or two of your unmet expectations with your group,

noting any themes that emerge among everyone's lists.

In the first part of her book, Missy noted several emotional reactions to the news about the health of her pregnancy with Mia, including feeling unsettled, unprepared, stunned, disbelieving, grief stricken, devastated, and also, later, *resolved*. When we come face-to-face with the realization that a core expectation we have held about life is at risk of not being met, big emotions like these tend to surface.

What about you? Review the list of unmet expectations your impossible burden represents, and then note the emotions you have experienced (and perhaps continue to experience) as a result on the following lines.

_____

_____

_____

Telling the Truth to God

In the introduction to her book, Missy says plainly that walking with God has been her sanity throughout every trial she has known. Knowing Him, trusting Him, crying out to Him when the outlook was bleak, and turning to her faith instead of caving in to fear and pain have proven to be the most valuable actions she could take. And just as she first discovered during her early days of ministry and marriage, one of the most profitable ways for us to know God is to read and meditate on His Word.

How would you describe your level of reliance on God's Word, the Bible, as you go about your day-to-day life? Check one of the following boxes.

☐ CONSTANT. I read it every day and can't imagine life without the guidance and encouragement it offers.

☐ OFTEN. I read the Bible from time to time but not every day.

☐ OCCASIONAL. During some seasons of my life, I've been known to read God's Word. But it's been awhile . . .

☐ RARE. Honestly, I've never really made a practice of reading the Bible.

What personal benefits would you hope to receive, or have you already received, as a result of increasing your faithfulness to reading God's Word, especially during burdensome times? Jot down your thoughts on the following lines. An example has been provided.

☐ Example: <u>A sense of peace, even when life feels chaotic</u> .

☐ _____.

☐ _____.

☐ _____.

☐ _____.

☐ _____.

In the pages of Scripture, we find people with hopes and dreams and sorrows similar to ours, people who also carried burdens that felt utterly impossible to bear. And as we watch them wrestle with their big emotions before God, we gain insights into how to win the knock-down, drag-out matches with fear and faithlessness that we ourselves sometimes face.

In the Old Testament book of Psalms, a handful of the entries are known as "psalms of lament," and here we find a treasure trove of lessons to be learned. In these particular psalms, the writers address God by describing all of the terrible things that are happening to them, as well as several reasons why God should quickly intervene. They then promise God that in exchange for a divine rescue operation, they and all of their fellow believers will offer praises of thanksgiving to their King. In other words, "Our lives are bad, but You, God, are good, so do something really good to make all our bad go away."

You probably can relate to this sentiment of wishing a good God would remove the bad parts of your life. Based on your impossible burden, what would such an exchange involve? Infertility for fertility? Insecurity for security? Despair for hope? On the following lines, note the bad things you wish God would remove and also the good things you wish He'd replace them with.

God, please take these bad things . . .	*and replace them with these that are good.*
_____	_____
_____	_____
_____	_____
_____	_____
_____	_____

Now take a look at the following excerpt from Psalm 44, one of the psalms of lament, circling all of the emotionally charged words and phrases you can find. A sample has been provided.

O God, we give glory to you all
    day long
  and constantly praise your
    name.
But now you have
    (tossed us aside)
    in dishonor.
  You no longer lead our
    armies to battle.
You make us retreat from our
    enemies
    and allow those who hate us
    to plunder our land.

You have butchered us like
    sheep
    and scattered us among the
    nations.
You sold your precious people
    for a pittance,
    making nothing on the sale.
You let our neighbors mock us.
  We are an object of scorn
    and derision to those
    around us.
You have made us the butt of
    their jokes;

they shake their heads at us
in scorn.
We can't escape the constant
humiliation;
shame is written across our
faces.
All we hear are the taunts of
our mockers.
All we see are our vengeful
enemies.

Wake up, O Lord! Why do you
sleep?

Get up! Do not reject us
forever.
Why do you look the other
way?
Why do you ignore
our suffering and
oppression?
We collapse in the dust,
lying face down in the dirt.
Rise up! Help us!
Ransom us because of your
unfailing love.

PSALM 44:8-16, 23-26

Want to read more? Go to the halfway point in your Bible, flip open to the book of Psalms, and devour the entries in any order you wish. The psalms you find here are some of the very first "worship choruses" ever sung. God's people would belt them out as they traveled on foot from one place to another, with or without instruments, as a way to stay connected to Him throughout their days. Whether you choose to sing the psalms, pray them, memorize them, or simply read them, you will always find your life richer after having let them enter your heart and mind.

The psalmists' bad-replaced-with-good grids would probably list exchanges such as these: dishonor for honor; rejection for acceptance; humiliation for admiration; and oppression for peace. If the writers were listing their emotions as you did on page 6, they would use hard-hitting words such as these:

☐ Tossed aside ☐ Dishonored ☐ Abandoned
☐ Butchered ☐ Scattered ☐ Mocked
☐ Scorned ☐ Humiliated ☐ Ashamed
☐ Taunted ☐ Oppressed ☐ Exhausted
☐ Hopeless ☐ Face-down-
      in-the-dirt
      afraid

Pretty strong language, right? (Feel free to check the boxes beside any words you wish you'd included, now that you know these types of reactions are totally acceptable.) The psalmists were *mad*, and they had no problem whatsoever admitting it. This is why it is helpful to read the Bible, by the way. In its pages and its themes, we are reminded that we never walk alone. We're not the only ones who have struggled, and just like the many faithful followers who have gone before us, we too can overcome.

The psalmists wouldn't stay mad forever; no, God had plans for them that were good. But before the psalmists got to those good things, they had to deal with the bad things, the burdens they truly believed were far too difficult for them to bear. Which brings us back to the impossible burden you are bearing: Maybe it's time to let God know how you feel, deep in your heart of hearts.

My Personal Song of Lament

The last few pages of chapter 3 in Missy's book form something of a psalm of lament. You'll recall that Missy was several weeks into her pregnancy with Mia and picked up the phone to receive troubling news from her doctor. Missy hadn't been given the necessary Rhogam shot administered to expectant mothers who have negative blood types. Because of this, she learned that her baby could face possible health challenges and birth defects. To make matters worse, her doctor seemed to lack compassion in delivering blow after blow of bad news and was stoic instead of responsive when Missy asked her how to proceed. Had Missy sat down on the heels of that phone call and penned her own official psalm—the lament part, anyway—it probably would have used words that express the same level of irritation as these do:

O God, I have sought to serve
    You all my days
  and constantly tried to do
    the right thing.
But now I am in this distressing
    situation,
    one that seems to get crazier
    day by day.

You are making this more
    difficult than it has
    to be;
    I feel completely abandoned.
You have left me without my
    Rhogam shot
  and have mounted the risks
    that I face.

You have put a C-section
before me,
   something You know *full
   well* I don't want to do.
I can't escape the constant
frustration;
   despair is written across my
   downcast face.
All I hear are voices that crush
my spirit, saying,
   "Sorry. There's nothing we
   can do."
Wake up, O Lord! What are
You doing up there?

Get up! Aren't You on my
side?
Why do You look the other
way?
Why do You ignore all my
hollering down here?
I'm about to utterly collapse in
the dust;
   You'll soon find me face
   down in the dirt.
Rise up, God! You can do this!
Come help me! Show me
how deep is Your love!

MISSY'S PSALM OF LAMENT

In our frustration, it's completely natural to point to other human beings as the source of our pain. If those people would just quit being awful and start being nice or quit being manipulative and start being honest or quit being unfair and start being just or quit being dismissive and start being responsible—*then* things would start to improve. Sometimes we even point to ourselves as the source of our angst.

> *If I could just stop sinning . . .*
> *If I could just start exercising . . .*
> *If I could just stop spending more than I make . . .*
> *If I could just start using my words wisely . . .*
> *If I could just stop holding a grudge . . .*
> *If I could just carry a baby to term . . .*

For Missy, it was her frustrating doctor who stood in the way of her realizing fulfillment and success—in terms of her pregnancy, anyway. For you, it may be your spouse or your in-laws or your sibling or your boss. It may be your child, your neighbor, your ex . . . or even you. Take a moment to consider who seems to be contributing to the weight of the impossible burden you bear. Is it a family member? A friend? A colleague? Your own body, heart, or mind?

Then, craft your own psalm (or "song") of lament, filling in the blanks as you go.

O God, I have sought to_____, and I have constantly tried to honor you by_____. But now you have given me this burden _____, which is making me crazier day by day. You are making this more difficult than it has to be by allowing _____. You have left me here without _____, and you have increased the _____ that I face. You have put _____ before me, something you know full well I don't want to do. You let _____ happen, and now I feel weak, alone, and afraid. I can't escape this constant feeling of _____ that is written all over my face. Wake up, Lord! Why do you leave me to _____ by myself? I am feeling utterly ____ _____. Please come rescue me quickly, Lord. Please don't ignore my cries for help!

+➤ WITH YOUR GROUP ➤+

Read your "song of lament" aloud to your group. Then
discuss the emotions you experienced while writing it.

The One Who Lifts Our Burdens

The Psalms remind us that even as we scan the horizon for someone to blame during our heavily burdened seasons of life, the only One who can really do anything to lift the weight that threatens to undo us is the ultimate Burden Lifter, God. Jesus said, "Come to me, all of you who are weary and carry heavy burdens, and I will give you rest" (Matthew 11:28). He knew this life would be burdensome. He knew we'd need a break. And so He provided a rest stop along our sometimes-exhausting journey, where we could refuel and gather ourselves. To our impossible burdens and too-big emotions and helpless feelings and hopeless nights, Jesus says, "I haven't left you. I haven't abandoned you. I haven't forgotten you. I still care. Hand over the burdens you've been trying to carry alone. I'll shoulder them from now on."

We look to our maddening doctor or mother-in-law or boss or spouse and beg the heavens to make them behave, while God waits patiently for us to discover that the solution we seek is found only in Him. Only Jesus can lift our impossible burden, leaving undeniable blessing in its place.

Certainly, the blessing that is left behind may look

different than the blessing we imagine. But what we often fail to realize is that *His* blessing is the only one that will satisfy our souls. Yes, He could choose to remove our burden altogether and send us on our way, free of our pain at last. But equally true is that He could allow the burden to persist, and through it bring great glory to Himself. We desperately want to weigh in on this vote, don't we? We want to beg God to go the first way. "Remove this impossible burden, God," we cry. "I can't bear it even one more hour." To which our loving Father meets our gaze with love in His eyes and says, "Child, you don't have to—don't you know? I'll bear your burden for you."

"Take my yoke upon you. Let me teach you, because I am humble and gentle at heart, and you will find rest for your souls. For my yoke is easy to bear, and the burden I give you is light" (Matthew 11:29-30). Ah, in the end, we aren't expected to carry our heavy burdens at all. Christ has come to lift them from the sagging shoulders on which they rest. And in their place, He offers His light burden, which is really no burden at all. The burden of walking with Jesus is a life of humility and gentleness and rest.

For Missy, the "beauty" that was left behind, once she allowed Christ to lift the burden she'd been carrying alone, was far different from the beauty she'd hoped for months before. Any mother would be anguished to watch her child endure multiple surgeries, procedures, pokes, prods, medications, and more. We want "easy" where our babies are concerned, and Mia's early days were anything but easy.

As you think about the paragraphs you've just read—about Jesus wanting to lift your burden and leave something beautiful, something that *blesses* you, in its place—what fears or insecurities start to surface in you? How does it make you feel to consider that His version of "beautiful" might be different from what you desire? Jot down your thoughts on the following lines, before moving on to part 2.

_____

_____

_____

_____

_____

_____

_____

_____

_____

_____

⚬— WITH YOUR GROUP —⚬

Discuss with your group why it often feels scary to let go of our need

for control and instead trust God's will and way for our lives.

Notes, Resolutions, Ponderings, and Such

PART II

Tell Your Truth

TO PREPARE FOR PART II,

PLEASE READ CHAPTERS 4, 5, AND 6

IN MISSY'S BOOK BLESSED, BLESSED . . . BLESSED.

～

I am glad to boast about my weaknesses, so that the power of Christ can work through me.

THE APOSTLE PAUL[2]

～

It has been said that only in togetherness is there strength, a concept strongly validated by the great cinematic classic *Finding Nemo.* Remember near the end of the movie, how Marlin and his pal Dory finally find Marlin's son, Nemo? Shortly after their long-awaited reunion, the threesome realizes that both Nemo and Dory have been caught in a giant fishing net, and unless radical action is taken, their terrible fate will be sealed. From outside the fishing net, Marlin hollers at the thousands of fish surrounding his son and Dory not to give up. "Just keep swimming," he says, a line he stole from Dory earlier in the movie. Dory starts echoing Marlin in her singsong voice—"Just keep swimming . . . just keep swimming . . . just keep swimming, swimming, swimming"—and eventually, the strategy works. The force of the huge school of fish swimming against the pull of the fishing net being hoisted to the surface of the water causes the net to burst apart, freeing all the enslaved fish.

It's just an imaginative kids' movie, admittedly, but that scene captures profound truth. When we choose community instead of isolation, progress tends to unfold. When we swim together and not apart, we find a way to live free.

We Need One Another

From Missy's earliest days of marriage and ministry, the concept of living in community—*with others* rather than isolated and alone—was prized. She and Jase decided early on to open their hearts and their home to the presence of other people longing to live for God. They held Bible studies, baptisms, and even a wedding in their living room, proof that they were serious about being connected instead of detached.

Missy admitted she was unsure whether she had anything to offer the people who gathered in her home. She was sheltered; they were worldly. She was naive; they were street smart. She was sober; they were recovering addicts. She was prudent; they were wild. Despite all the differences, however, Jase encouraged Missy to plow ahead. He convinced her that God would not have brought to them anyone whom they could not somehow help, and so Missy began watching for ways God was knitting the group's hearts together—the ways they could indeed help one another live well.

∞

Think about your own journey thus far. When have you known the power of living in life-giving community? Perhaps a friend or a group of friends has come alongside you during a challenging situation. Or maybe coworkers once pitched in to cover your shifts when you were recovering from an illness of some sort. Did a neighbor or a friend from church drop off homemade soup when your child was sick? Did family members send e-mails to let you know they were praying for you during a difficult time? Choose one of your community-oriented memories. Then, on the following lines, recount the situation. What was the circumstance you faced? Who pitched in to help? What action did they take? How did it make you feel?

_____

_____

_____

_____

⤞ WITH YOUR GROUP ⤝

Discuss with the other members of your group what "authentic community" looks and feels like when it's working right.

Once we find the courage to name our impossible burden and declare it to God, as you were led to do in part 1, we then face the sometimes-daunting task of sharing that burden with real, live, in-the-flesh people who can help. The reason for this is simple: We are better together than apart. (Remember Nemo?) In fact, the Bible contains example after example of ways that we can do life together so that none of us ever walks alone.

First, look up the five passages that follow, either in your own Bible or by reading the left side of the grid (these verses are from the New Living Translation). Then, note on the right what you learn about how we are to support one another in practical ways.

SCRIPTURE REFERENCE	PRACTICAL WAYS WE CAN SUPPORT ONE ANOTHER
Romans 15:7—"Accept each other just as Christ has accepted you so that God will be given glory."	
Galatians 6:2—"Share each other's burdens, and in this way obey the law of Christ."	
Hebrews 10:25—"Let us not neglect our meeting together, as some people do, but encourage one another, especially now that the day of his return is drawing near."	
James 5:16—"Confess your sins to each other and pray for each other so that you may be healed. The earnest prayer of a righteous person has great power and produces wonderful results."	

In total, there are *fifty-nine* of these statements in Scripture about practical ways we can come alongside another person and walk with him or her, especially during difficult times. This concept was obviously important to God, or else He wouldn't have peppered it so frequently throughout His

Word. We really are better together—especially when times get tough. But here's the key to all this togetherness: We have to first let people in. We have to be willing to tell the truth about our situations if we ever expect others to help.

As you read chapters 4, 5, and 6 of *Blessed, Blessed . . . Blessed* in preparation for working through this part of the journal, you may have noticed how Missy was accompanied by many family members, friends, and acquaintances while on her difficult journey, all of whom upheld her and spurred her on. For instance,

> ⇢ *during her pregnancy with Mia and through the multiple doctor and specialist appointments, her family and friends prayed with Jase and her;*
>
> ⇢ *her mother-in-law, sisters-in-law, and sons accompanied her to her ultrasound, where she first saw Mia's face;*
>
> ⇢ *Jase's cousin Melissa, a trained speech therapist, advised Missy in those early, fearful days of not knowing how to prepare for Mia's arrival;*
>
> ⇢ *her brother-in-law communicated with the congregation of their church about the concerns Jase and Missy had about Mia's care;*
>
> ⇢ *her sister-in-law and other friends took it upon themselves to decorate Mia's nursery;*
>
> ⇢ *countless friends and family members waited eagerly in the hospital waiting room while Mia was being born;*
>
> ⇢ *her parents kept her two boys for her while she recovered from her C-section;*

→ *various nurses and hospital staff made sure Missy and Mia were cared for at every turn;*

→ *doctors, specialists, and surgeons ensured that Mia received their best energies and expertise;*

→ *and a whole host of other families became instant friends, based on their shared cleft-lip-and-palate journeys.*

This list could go on. And while you might not realize it just yet, *a similar list is waiting for you, once you boldly tell your truth.*

Had Missy holed away and cut herself off from friends and family members, opting instead to "go it alone," she never would have been the recipient of all that love, concern, and care. In the same way, as you carefully invite a handful of trusted friends and family members into the burden you find yourself carrying, you will discover that a whole line of loved ones is eager to help you live weightlessly by encouraging you to trust God, day by day.

→ WITH YOUR GROUP →

When the pressure is on, are you more likely to rush toward your beloved friends and ask for support, or to hole away and try to solve problems on your own? Or does it depend on the nature of the circumstance? Discuss your thoughts with your group.

Whom to Trust with Your Truth

Whether the burden you bear is financial, emotional, spiritual, physical, vocational, or relational in nature, there are people *already in your life* who can lend supportive hands or listening ears. You don't have to walk this path alone. We are better together, right? For instance, as you consider your various relationship spheres—friends, family members, colleagues, neighbors, and such—whose face pops to the surface of your thoughts when you think of adjectives such as *trustworthy, discreet, attentive, others focused,* and *kind*? This type of person makes a great confidant—someone you can trust to keep your struggle confidential, someone who will help you with quiet assistance and prayer.

You probably have a few adjectives of your own that you're looking for as you consider telling the truth of your pain. On the following lines, note the descriptors that need to be true of a friend or family member before you would feel secure sharing the burden you bear.

My confidant(s) must be . . .

_____

_____

_____

Next, spend a few moments asking God to reveal the people in your sphere of influence who embody those characteristics you wrote down. On the following lines, list the names of your potential confidants, the people who could make up your "support team."

My Potential Support Team

_____   _____

_____   _____

_____   _____

_____   _____

Finally, as you look over the list of names you've created, put a circle around the three or four people who really stand out to you as being true supporters, people who are most likely to help you walk this path you're on.

∞

Here is where the rubber meets the road, because for most people, the idea of sharing their deepest struggle is one thing, but the execution of that idea is quite another. It's *hard* to let people see where we hurt, even people we consider the closest of friends. Surely you can relate. Maybe you have confided private information to someone who then sneakily shared it with someone else. Maybe upon confiding in a family member, your self-disclosure was met not with compassion, but with judgment or scorn. Along the way, it's possible you've lost a friendship, a job, or something else you held dear—all because you chose to tell the truth of a tough situation you were in. Think back on your life's experiences as they relate to sharing confidences with trusted loved ones. Then note an occasion when you confided in someone and had that situation come back to bite you in the end.

I confided in someone I thought I could trust,
and then this happened . . .

_____

_____

_____

_____

> ⊷ **WITH YOUR GROUP** ⊶
>
> *Without naming names—in other words, be discreet!—discuss*
> *a time when a confidence of yours was broken and you felt*
> *betrayed as a result. On the flip side, when have you spoken out*
> *of turn about another person's troubles and later regretted saying*
> *what you said? Describe the experiences for your group.*

Being bitten can hurt. Especially when the one biting you is someone you thought you could trust. This is why it is so crucial to spend significant time asking God for insight regarding the specific person or people who can help you carry the burden you bear. In the Bible, God promises to give wisdom to everyone who asks for it (see James 1:5). One of the best things you can do is to pray, "God, please increase my wisdom as I seek out trusted friends. I know it is unwise to walk alone through a difficult season, so please direct my steps toward the small group of people who can help me most."

God loves to answer this type of request.

∾

It is true: Being in community with other mistake-making human beings can cause us loads of pain and angst. But the opposite is also true: When we open ourselves up to sojourning with flesh-and-blood brothers and sisters, we stand to make *great* gains. Remember, at the beginning of this part, you noted a life-giving experience that came to you courtesy of letting others into your journey along the way. You'll also recall that in terms of Missy's story, she never would have been in touch with the stellar surgeon who served Mia and their family so well had she not allowed her church family to come alongside her during her time of deepest need. We really are better together, which is why God elevates the ideals of unity and togetherness, of compassion and self-sacrifice and love.

Given the specific burden you will be sharing with those superstars you circled on your potential support team (page

30), what benefits do you hope to realize once you take that colossal step of faith? For Missy, a key benefit she realized upon telling her truth to others was a very practical medical resource for her daughter. For you, it may look very different from that. Do you hope for emotional support, such as a knowing smile or a caring phone call from time to time? Or is it financial support you need, such as help with groceries or tips for managing a budget for the first time? Maybe you need practical helps, such as babysitting assistance or tutoring for your floundering grade-school child. Perhaps your need is spiritual in nature—someone you can pray with any time, day or night. Jot down the benefits you hope to realize in the space provided.

_____

_____

_____

_____

_____

These desires of your heart can be formed into a prayer to God that has been started for you on page 35. Ask Him to work through the lives of the people you know and to provide the resources He knows you most need. If you are serious about prizing community in the manner He instructs in His Word, then tell Him so. If you are committed to trusting Him fully as He causes beauty to spring forth from all your pain, tell Him that, too. (More on "trusting God" in part 3 . . . stay tuned.) Speak to Him as your loving Father— He is eager to be that for you.

If you don't yet know God as Father—and as Savior and Lord—you can surrender to His leadership even now. Review the following prayer, and if you mean every word of it in your heart of hearts, then repeat that prayer to God.

PRAYER OF SURRENDER TO CHRIST

Dear Jesus, today I want to stop going my own way in life and start going Your way instead. I recognize and freely admit to You that I have sinned against You and have fallen short of Your standard of holiness for me. Please forgive me. I want to pursue peace—in relationship to You, and in the depth of my heart. Please come into my heart and cleanse me from my wrongdoing. Make me brand-new. Fill me with Your Holy Spirit. I give You complete access to all of me. By faith, I know that You hear my prayer, that You have saved me from my sin, and that You are committed to transforming me into the person I was designed to be. Thank You for loving me. In Your name I pray, amen.

Dear heavenly Father,

_____

_____

_____

_____

_____

_____

_____

Amen.

Speaking Up at Last

In chapter 6, Missy said that the day she and her family spent at Medical City in Dallas during which newborn Mia was seen by specialist after specialist was the most traumatic day she had ever known. And yet even on that day beautiful blessings awaited her, for the simple reason that she had not allowed herself to go through that day alone. "One of the unexpected joys of our ride home that evening," she wrote, "was that my parents and Miss Kay were full of stories about people they had met in waiting rooms throughout the day. It seemed as though they encountered the people we needed to share with us their success stories, provide information and opinions on certain doctors, and talk about what to expect as Mia progressed on her journey."

That day represented a breaking point for Missy, and yet because she had surrounded herself with a team of supporters, she did not break apart. The same will be true for us all, as we invite others into our pain. In part 3, we will explore the type of help you should request from your support system, but for now, go ahead and commit to trusting a small group of people with your truth. Determine in your heart that you will speak up, and in due time you will see God do amazing things through those intimate chats.

⊱ WITH YOUR GROUP ⊰

If you haven't yet confided in a trusted friend the reality of the burden you're carrying, then discuss what has kept you from doing so. If you have, then discuss the benefits of companionship you've known thus far.

Notes, Resolutions, Ponderings, and Such

PART III

Grow as You Go

TO PREPARE FOR PART III,

PLEASE READ CHAPTERS 7, 8, AND 9

IN MISSY'S BOOK BLESSED, BLESSED . . . BLESSED.

Now we see things imperfectly, like puzzling reflections in a mirror, but then we will see everything with perfect clarity. All that I know now is partial and incomplete, but then I will know everything completely, just as God now knows me completely.

THE APOSTLE PAUL[3]

If you've ever watched an NFL football game, then you know the sport isn't for the faint of heart. It's unforgiving, hard-hitting, and by some standards, downright violent. NFL quarterbacks are especially vulnerable to powerful takedowns because they are the ones who have the ball at the beginning of every play. And when a three hundred–pound defenseman sees the quarterback with the ball and comes charging toward him in an all-out effort to strip it from his hands, a collision is sure to occur. Regardless of how strong the quarterback is, how thick his shoulder pads are, and how braced he is for the hit, tackles almost always hurt. Which is why it is so interesting and unusual that one of the league's most promising quarter-backs actually *thanks* defenders for their hardest hits.

Andrew Luck has been the starting quarterback for the Indianapolis Colts since 2012 and has thrown for more yards in his first three years than any other quarterbacks in history have during their initial three. The guy is *good*. And because he is good, opposing teams' defenders bring their A-games each time they face him. But what is astounding is that when one of their hits connects and Luck is taken down, Luck doesn't cuss them out or holler at the referee for a penalty flag to be thrown. Instead he says, "Wow, great job! What a *hit*. Nice work."

Defenders never know what to say in response. One of them, a player for the New England Patriots, was so baffled by the compliments he received after sacking Luck one time that before racing over to his team to prepare for the next play, he turned toward the cheerful quarterback and stammered, "Thanks for . . . uh . . . accepting that hit?"[4]

It's tough to know what to do with someone who stays fired up after he's been knocked down.

→ WITH YOUR GROUP ←

On the "optimism/pessimism" scale, how optimistic would your closest friends say you are, even when life's circumstances are tough to manage? How optimistic would you say you are? Are you pleased with your self-assessment here? Discuss your thoughts with the group.

Even the Tough Tend to Grumble

When life feels hard and our burdens threaten to take us down, cheerfulness and optimism seem to be a million miles away. This is why Andrew Luck's approach seems so out of place to us: We don't expect happiness in the face of hard hits, but rather a fair amount of grimacing and gripes.

Surely you can relate—even the most optimistic among us can. When you are most in touch with the irritation, inconvenience, awfulness, and pain of the impossible burden you've acknowledged, what does your own version of "grumbling" sound like? If your burden is financial in nature, perhaps you grumble about how expensive everything is or how unfair it is that another person doing the same job as you is making more money. If your burden is relational in nature, maybe your grumbling centers on how the other person needs to change. If it's a medical situation that has you stymied, you may grumble in your darker moments about how unjust it is that you eat healthfully and exercise regularly and have nothing more to show for it than the awful diagnosis you were given. Take a minute to get in touch with your inner grumbler, and then note the themes you tend to grumble about on the following lines.

_____

_____

_____

Grumbling can feel so good, can't it? And yet you've probably noticed by now that nothing useful comes from it. Grumbling squelches all the good stuff—things such as optimism, positive energy, and hope. Sure, it may feel good in the moment to unload our frustrations and lay out our complaints, but as soon as that moment passes, we're more deflated than we were to start.

What adjectives best describe how you feel after you grumble (to yourself or to others) about your tough situation? Write them on the following lines.

Grumbling feels good in the moment, but afterward, I feel . . .

_____

_____

_____

Now that you have taken pains to name your burden (part 1 of this guide) and also to declare your support team so that you don't have to walk this journey toward wholeness alone (part 2), it's time to sort out what to say to ourselves and to others as we talk through the burdens we bear. Sure, we can complain until the cows come home, but perhaps there is a wiser, more profitable way to invest our energies and our words. Maybe instead of grumbling we can actually *grow* as we go.

The Choice: To Grumble or Grow

There are essentially two responses to the realization that life is not meeting our expectations: We can grumble, or else we can grow. We've explored the grumbling side of the equation; now let's discover how to grow.

Growth Strategy #1: Try On Joy

The Bible includes an interesting invitation to everyone facing the tough stuff of life. In Romans 5, the apostle Paul (who under the inspiration of the Holy Spirit authored the book) begins by talking about the peace we have in God because of Jesus Christ's sacrifice for humankind, when He suffered and died on the cross. Paul says that if we have faith in God that is born of trusting in the finished work of Christ, we can live every single day of our lives "confidently" and "joyfully," as we "look forward to sharing God's glory" someday (verse 2).

What Paul is talking about here is the reality that for everyone who knows and loves God and seeks to serve Him all their days, once their earthly life comes to a conclusion, they will spend eternity right by God's side. If you devote yourself to God, He will forever devote Himself to you. It's a powerful proposition indeed.

So Paul presents this compelling backdrop—that when you live for Christ, confidence and joy can be yours—and then dives a little deeper, just to make sure we catch his point. Take a look at Romans 5:3-5 in the callout and circle every positive-sounding noun that you find. (In case being quizzed on English grammar feels terrifying, a couple of them have been circled for you.)

We can rejoice, too, when we run into problems and trials, for we know that they help us develop endurance. And endurance develops strength of character, and character strengthens our confident hope of salvation. And this hope will not lead to disappointment. For we know how dearly God loves us, because he has given us the Holy Spirit to fill our hearts with his love" (Romans 5:3-5).

On the day when Missy saw the first 4-D ultrasound image of Mia and realized that something regarding her baby's facial structure was not as it should be, Jase tried to encourage her by saying, "We'll just have to teach her that beauty is on the inside." Missy was understandably too shaken by the news of Mia's cleft lip and palate to fully appreciate Jase's words just then, but in reflecting on the power of them she later said, "They have been a source of strength and a lifeline for me in many different situations we have been through with Mia. I hated them when he said them; I cherish them now."

Guess what Jase was doing as he uttered those cherished words. He was trying on joy.

Of course he was rattled by the news of the challenges his baby girl would face.

Of course he was in a state of disbelief over what this turn of events would mean for his family's life.

Of course he felt the financial strain as he mentally tallied all the expenses that would come.

Of course he was worried for Missy, who felt incredulous and sad and alone.

Of course his inner grumbler was gearing up to whoop and holler about how unfair it all was.

But when Jase Robertson opened his lips to speak, what came out of his mouth was *joy.*

Despite the countless negative emotions begging him to try them on for size, he chose instead to try on joy. *We can make the same choice too.*

"We can," the apostle Paul says at the start of verse 3. "We can rejoice . . . when we run into problems and trials." As crazy as it may sound to us, we can stay fired up even when we're knocked down.

Perhaps you're open to giving it a try?

On the left-hand side of the following grid, copy down the themes of grumbling you noted on page 43. Then, on the right, jot down what a joyful response might sound like, even if you don't yet *feel* very joyful inside. An example has been provided for you.

THE NO-JOY THEMES OF MY GRUMBLING	WHAT I MIGHT SAY IF I GAVE JOY A TRY
Ex. "Why is everyone able to find a job but me?"	"I have skills to offer someone. Now I just need to sort out where, exactly, that someone is."

⊹ WITH YOUR GROUP ⊹

Read one of your before-and-after entries from the grid aloud to your group. How does the joyful response feel as it rolls off your tongue? Can you see yourself adopting a posture of greater joy going forward? Why or why not? Discuss your thoughts with the group.

An interesting thing happens when we choose to try on joy: The world around us starts to feel a little less horrible and bleak. We see *beauty* peeking out from behind even the most terrible trials we face. On the day of her baby's first surgery, when Mia was barely three months old, Missy happened to notice in the pre-op waiting area a fully decorated Christmas tree that boasted on its branches stuffed teddy bears of every color and size. A nurse explained to Missy that the bears had been placed there by a generous soul who wanted to be sure that every child who was due for surgery during the holidays that year would have a stuffed friend to take along.

It would have been easy for Missy not to notice the beauty of that tree. Who has time to take in the hospital's holiday decorations when your baby girl is going under the knife? But not only did she stop and soak in the twinkling lights and stuffed friends, she also let the gesture penetrate her defenses and minister to her weary heart. "Knowing that someone was thoughtful enough to care about patients and families facing surgery during the holidays meant so much to me," she later wrote. "I loved the fact that Mia had a new teddy bear for her big day."

Depending on your level of despondence over the burden you think you just can't bear, this next exercise may seem awkward to you. But regardless of where you are on your journey from feeling *heavily burdened* to feeling *blessed*, the suggestion stands: Declare the beauty in your situation, even as that situation is admittedly hard. Where are the twinkling lights in your world right now, the stuffed animals, the generous souls? Take a few moments to think about the glimpses of goodness that are lighting your shadowy path these days, and then note them on the following lines as reminders that *all is not dark*. There is always a hint of light to be found, if we only have eyes to see it.

_____

_____

_____

_____

> ⮞ **WITH YOUR GROUP** ⮜
>
> *What is one glimmer of light that is reminding you these days*
> *that despite your difficult burden, all is not dark in your world?*
> *What habits or realities in your life tend to keep you from*
> *noticing the beauty peeking out from behind the pain?*

When we lift our heads even momentarily and take in the small but bright lights that are illuminating our way, we discover that even though we're weary and wrung dry, somehow we can take another step. Like driving through the fog, as long as we can see a teeny bit of road in front of us, we can carefully roll ahead another mile.

This is what the apostle Paul knew and that we're still trying to grasp in our day: By choosing to see the joyous and the beautiful and the wise, we have the opportunity to carve out new capacities for endurance that we never knew we had. And as Romans 3:4 tells us, endurance is what leads to character, and the development of character is what leads to hope. This brings us to our next growth strategy. Once we have a little endurance on our side, we can baby-step our way along.

Growth Strategy #2: Take a Useful Step

You've probably seen the following dynamic play out first-hand. You face a troubling situation and think there is *no way* you can overcome the pressure and tension and pain. But then something happens that gives you strength for the day, and you wake up the next morning thinking, *I can't believe I made it through yesterday.*

That day, something else happens to give you a few puffs of courage and strength, and you wake up the following morning thinking, *It happened again. Somehow, I made it through another day.*

You string together a couple of days, then a few weeks, and then, astoundingly, a *month*. Before you know it, you have survived a stressful season. The worry that was suffocating you is now lifting ever so slightly, and finally you feel like you can take a deep breath. Never in a million years would you have guessed that you could get over that obstacle, but somehow, some way, you made it.

And look at you now. *You've overcome.*

Take a few minutes to reflect on the most difficult obstacles you've had to overcome across the years and decades of your life. (A handful of examples in the following callout might help spark your memory.) Then, on the following lines, jot down one or two of the more challenging experiences that come to mind, noting what happened, how you responded, and the results you saw come to pass.

Victories Worth Celebrating
→ *Wholeness after loss of a family member*

→ *Health after disease or obesity*

→ *Marital unity after infidelity*

→ *Hope after a miscarriage*

→ *Financial peace after bankruptcy*

→ *Pregnancy after infertility*

→ *Employment after job loss*

→ *Sobriety after substance abuse*

Victories I've Known

_____

_____

_____

_____

_____

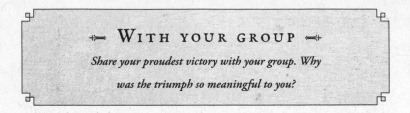

These situations aren't tidy—far from it. They are messy and overwhelming and can leave us feeling steamrollered flat. But we can prevail, can't we? In fact, *so many people do.* We and others whom we know walk through unthinkable circumstances all the way to the other side, where the sun is shining warmly once more. And the key to all those successes is that little idea of walking—day by day, moment by moment, step by step. We keep putting one foot in front of the other, believing that simple progress will lead to success.

∞

Choose one of the obstacles you overcame, from the list on page 51. If you were to rewind your victory back to the very beginning, what would you say was the *first step* you took toward springing free from the struggle you were in? It may seem trivial to you now, given hindsight, but as you look back, you can see the profound effects the action had on you and on the situation at hand.

For Missy, one of the simplest steps she took during the trying time when nine-year-old Mia was given headgear to wear was to devote herself to ensuring that Mia wore it and to rally her own support team to pray it would help.

For you, the "simple first step" that led to your victory may have been a change in attitude. Or signing up for a class. Or saying, "That's it. No more." It may have been cutting up your credit cards. Or emptying the wine bottles into the sink. Or calling to say, "I'm sorry." Or going for a half-mile jog. What was the first simple step for you? Jot it down on the lines provided. Then explain why it mattered.

If you'll recall, that first step you took led to another simple step, which led to another step right after that. And eventually you found yourself standing at a place called "victory," or "all rightness," or "peace," even as you couldn't believe you were there. This is how it works with steps of progress. Eventually, we make our way through.

So, what is the step you know you need to take this time around to help lift the current burden you bear? We usually know the answer to this question, even as we hesitate to tell the truth. If you're feeling especially bold at the moment, write your answer on the following lines.

The Step I Need to Take Now . . . and Why

_____

_____

_____

_____

_____

_____

_____

⤙ WITH YOUR GROUP ⤚

No surprise here: Tell your group the step you wish to take. Afterward,

be sure to let them know how they can support

you as you make that leap of faith.

Your first steps toward hope and healing may be taken on legs that are shaky and weak, but given where they will lead you, the wobbles will be well worth it in the end.

Growth Strategy #3: Trust God

The third growth strategy is the one that holds the other two together, for it is only by trusting God—the One who created us and is committed to loving us and sustaining us—that we can know joy and make noteworthy progress in this life. (If, in your enthusiasm to dive into this journal, you blew past "A Note from Missy" on page *v*, take a few minutes to read it now.) As you consider the idea of trusting God for your ability to see your impossible burden lifted, what thoughts come to mind? Answer the following three questions before moving ahead.

1. *What does trusting God have to do with a person's ability to overcome the challenge he or she faces?*

2. *What practical steps would a person take who wanted to trust God for provision and peace more fully?*

3. *When have you sensed firsthand the provision and peace of God?*

⇥ **WITH YOUR GROUP** ⇤

Share your experience of knowing the provision and peace
of God from question 3. Also, discuss your thoughts on these
two questions: What did the experience teach you about God?
And what did the experience teach you about yourself?

Missy's first visit to Medical City with Mia thrust her into a grieving process that would take her years to fully work through. As she explained in her book, her grief wasn't over the loss of a person, but rather over the loss of a perception— the perception of a "perfect life." Grieving is neither easy nor quick, but for Missy, the beautiful byproduct of her grieving was that it led her to a sense of acceptance of Mia's challenges, and ultimately to a powerful "aha" moment, which we'll explore more fully. But first, let's consider that "sense of acceptance." On the scale of acceptance that follows, place an X to denote where you believe you stand today, with respect to denying or accepting the circumstances that are causing you grief.

Betrayal/Denial   Acceptance/Search for Solutions

┌───┐
│   ⇥ WITH YOUR GROUP ⇤   │
│   │
│   *Explain why you placed your X where you did on the acceptance* │
│   *continuum. Are you pleased with where you are in terms* │
│   *of coming to accept your circumstances as they are? Why or* │
│   *why not? Discuss your thoughts with your group.* │
└───┘

Now to the "aha" moment, or "epiphany," as Missy referred to it in chapter 7. In her words, "My personal journey of processing grief took me beyond acceptance to something even more powerful. I had an epiphany—a principle I knew intellectually suddenly became a deep conviction in my heart. I learned in a whole new way that what we view as perfection is not what God views as perfection. He sees us and our situations much differently than we do. From His perspective, not only was Mia perfect, our family's life and the plan He had for our future were perfect too."

For Missy, the epiphany was a shift in perspective—from what she had deemed acceptable or "perfect" to what God was saying was *already right.*

Depending on where you placed yourself on the continuum of acceptance, it may strike you as either a horrible proposition or else as an immensely comforting thought to realize that your present "impossible burden" could actually be part of God's perfect ("already right") plan. Why do you suppose it is so difficult for us human beings to accept what seem to be glaring imperfections in our lives as part of God's perfect plan? Jot down your thoughts in the space provided.

On viewing imperfections as perfect . . .

_____

_____

_____

The epigraph at the beginning of part 3 is from 1 Corinthians 13. The apostle Paul, writing under inspiration of the Holy Spirit says, "Now we see things imperfectly, like puzzling reflections in a mirror, but then we will see everything with perfect clarity. All that I know now is partial and incomplete, but then I will know everything completely, just as God now knows me completely" (verse 12).

It is true: When we are bearing impossible burdens, it feels as though we're trying to put together a puzzle without having the box top to tell us what the finished image will be. For Missy, her "puzzle pieces" may have included her tubal pregnancy, the pain of a botched operation, Rh incompatibility, an unmerciful and unkind doctor, the diagnosis of Mia's cleft lip and palate, financial stress, and later, Mia's oral devices—her headgear, multiple surgeries, and more. Why had God allowed these dramatic and unfortunate pieces into Missy's life, and what picture was He ultimately creating? Puzzling, indeed.

Consider the dynamics surrounding your impossible burden, all of the seemingly random situations and details that have mounted along the way. Name a handful of them on the following lines.

_____

_____

_____

It is no accident that our disparate puzzle pieces form a whole heart. In fact, that is what God is after. He allows all sorts of experiences—blessings, yes, but also tests and trials along the way—so that we will seek Him, know Him, praise Him, and depend on Him every moment of every day. And while we can't know the fullness of His methods just yet—while we still see things "imperfectly" or "dimly," as some Bible translations say—there will come a day of complete restoration, when we will suffer and grieve no more. And on that day, we will see more clearly how God worked in our lives, and why.

⇥ WITH YOUR GROUP ⇤

Discuss with your group members why God chooses not to reveal everything to us now and why He allows so many questions to go unanswered in our lives this side of heaven.

Spend a few moments thinking about that day when your vision will be corrected and you will see things from God's point of view, when the impossible burden you carry right now will be contextualized and better understood. On that day, you'll look back on this season of suffering, and you'll finally be able to see some of God's purposes in allowing it to take place in your life. On that day, many questions will at last have answers, and sorrows will be replaced with full joy. On that day, all that aches inside of you will be healed with fulfillment in Christ. What a day it will be. What's more, the total trust we easily place in God on that day is something we can begin practicing here and now. *We can practice trusting God now*, even with our imperfect vision.

Take another look at the "puzzling pieces" you noted on page 59. In the following prayer, fill in the blanks with the three most puzzling aspects of your situation. Then pray the entire prayer to God, either silently or aloud, asking Him to help you trust Him with the pieces of your burden that just don't make sense for now.

Heavenly Father,
Thank You for inviting me to come to You in prayer
and for promising to hear Your children's cries each time
they call out for help. I'm calling out for help today. This
burden has defined me far too long, and I am ready to
release it to Your care. I want to trust You instead of

trying to control everything myself. The truth is that I don't control anything very well. You are the only One who is good at being God, and so I willingly step aside and tell You that I trust You to care for me.

Specifically, I release to You the more puzzling parts of this situation, including

(1) _____,

(2) _____,

(3) _____.

I commit myself to practicing joy, to taking the useful steps of growth You prompt me to take, and to trusting You to bring beauty from this impossible burden I bear.

Thank You for knowing me and for loving me. Thank You for perfecting me day by day.

In Jesus' name I pray,

Amen.

Remember the support system you named on page 30, the people you are trusting to help you make it through this difficult time? Now that you see the benefits of trying on joy, taking helpful steps of action, and trusting God with your pain, be sure to tell them what you're learning and ask them for their help. Explain why you want to practice joyfulness even in the midst of great trials, and encourage them to tell you when they detect a joyful tone to your speech. Let them know the steps of action you feel called to take so that they can spur you on toward health and growth. Show them how you're working to trust God with the puzzling aspects of your situation, and enlist their prayer support. Your support team will receive the richest of blessings as you let them see you bearing your burden well.

No Regrets

Looking back on her family's journey thus far, Missy says that adjusting her attitude from one of defeat to one of victory, taking decisive steps of action to care for her daughter's multiple needs, and trusting God to provide the strength and courage she needed at every turn have made all the difference in the world. Remember that one specific, tangible fruit of her labors here involved Mia's jaw moving not one millimeter, as Mia's orthodontist had hoped for as a result of Mia's wearing her headgear, but a full *ten millimeters*, which broke every record the orthodontist's patients had held. Missy never would have signed up for putting her precious daughter through all of the pain, discomfort, inconvenience, and irritation that Mia's special needs have led to along the way, but upon accepting the circumstances *as they were* instead of how Missy *wished they would be*, she was able to see with fresh perspective God's faithfulness in providing just the progress they needed. Rather than grumble in her situation, she chose to grow from it, a move she never will regret.

The same can be true of us, if only we will allow ourselves

to grow. In part 1 of this book, all the way back on page 9, you noted a series of exchanges that you wished God would make on your behalf—"good things" He would insert in place of "bad things" that were making life rough. Copy a few of those "good things" on the following lines.

_____

_____

_____

_____

_____

Next, with that list of "good things" fresh on your mind, take a look at a sampling from Missy's list, being sure to notice whose name has been placed on top.

<u>GOD</u>

Perfectly healthy daughter.

No more surprises, no more pain.

Relief from medical expenses.

Compassionate doctor.

What Missy discovered along the way is that all of the "good things" she was pining for were actually arrows pointing her back to God. In her heart of hearts, what she wanted more than perfect health for Mia or relief from financial strain was *God*—His companionship, His compassion, His care. In fact, every need we know in this lifetime points to our deeper need for God. And as we pursue deeper intimacy with our heavenly Father, we craft a life for ourselves devoid of regret.

Review the list of good things you noted on the previous page. What questions, concerns, or insecurities come to mind as you consider writing "God" on top of your list? Do you really believe that the good things you seek are ultimately found only in Him? Why or why not? What words would you use in expressing your thoughts to God now? Spend some time on page 65 journaling about these topics before moving on to the fourth and final part of this guide, where we'll explore the blessings God wishes to give us and how to have open hands with which to receive them.

⇥ WITH YOUR GROUP ⇤

What do you make of the remark, "Every need we know in this lifetime points to our deeper need for God"? Talk with your group about the firsthand experiences and assumptions that influence your perspective here.

Notes, Resolutions, Ponderings, and Such

PART IV
Say Yes to "Blessed"

TO PREPARE FOR PART IV,

PLEASE READ CHAPTERS 10, 11, AND 12

IN MISSY'S BOOK BLESSED, BLESSED . . . BLESSED.

~

*May the Lord bless you and protect you. May the Lord
smile on you and be gracious to you. May the Lord show
you his favor and give you his peace.*

THE PRIESTLY BLESSING GIVEN TO THE PROPHET MOSES[1]

~

At the end of part 3, we looked at the idea that while our deepest desire is to have our impossible burden removed from our lives altogether, God's deepest desire is that we would *desire Him*, in the midst of our pain. It's sort of like that children's song of old, "Going on a Bear Hunt." Do you remember the lyrics to that song?

> *We're goin' on a bear hunt. (We're goin' on a bear hunt.)*
> *We're goin' to catch a big one. (We're goin' to catch a*
>   *big one.)*
> *I'm not scared. (I'm not scared.)*
> *What a beautiful day! (What a beautiful day!)*

After that opening chorus, a series of stanzas follow that reflect all the obstacles faced on that bear hunt—long, wavy grass; a deep, cold river; thick, oozy mud; a big, dark forest; and a swirling, whirling snowstorm—and with each obstacle comes this singsong reminder: "We can't go over it! We can't go under it! Oh no! We've got to go through it!"

This is exactly how we feel when we look at our impossible burden, isn't it? We say to God, "Can I please go over it? Or under it? Or maybe around it, just this once?" even as we know in our heart of hearts that we're probably going to have to march right on through it.

Others Who Had to Go through It

We're not the only ones who have found our burden way too much to bear and begged God to take it away. On the following grid, note the person you find in each Scripture passage and the specific burden that person begged God to remove.

BIBLE PASSAGE	WHO BORE THE BURDEN	THE BURDEN HE BORE
Numbers 11:10-15		
Job 7:11-16		
Luke 22:39-44		
2 Corinthians 12:1-10		

There is a precedent throughout Scripture of God asking His followers not to go over or under their difficult circumstances, but to go right *through* them instead. But another precedent is set there as well, which is that God never leaves them to walk through those burdens alone.

⊶ WITH YOUR GROUP ⊷

What comfort do you find in knowing that some of the people in the Bible that God worked through most profoundly also had impossible burdens to bear?

Just as the apostle Paul noted in the 2 Corinthians passage you looked up a moment ago, we can trust that God's strength is made known in our weakness; it is when we're utterly dependent on Him that He shows Himself strong. Now, in case you don't believe this to be true, check out the following set of Scriptures, jotting down the powerful outcomes that came out of the weaknesses of Moses, Job, Paul, and Jesus Christ.

BIBLE PASSAGE	HOW GOD SHOWED HIS STRENGTH
Exodus 14:21-22	
Job 42:12-17	
Philippians 2:5-11	
Philippians 4:10-14	

Throughout Missy and Mia's ordeal, for example, God has shown Himself strong by instilling in Mia a sense of unwavering tenacity to face excruciating challenges and prevail. She is one tough cookie, courtesy of the God who knew she would need to be. The same is true for you: If you were to spend some time contemplating your journey, you'd surely discover

God's strength there too. *Anytime* a lover of God experiences weakness, that is where God shows His strength. As we've seen in the first three parts of this journal, the hidden blessing behind every burden is that God's power is made known in our impotence. Our "can't" always equals God's "can."

Now, if only we'd remember that truth. *If only we'd live as though that truth were true.*

⤖ WITH YOUR GROUP ⤖

Describe a time when you faced a serious "can't" but watched God turn it into a "can." What emotions did you experience when you witnessed your heavenly Father making a way for you, where by your assessment there was absolutely no way *before?*

We Need to Be Reminded

Evidently, we're not the only ones who are forgetful when it comes to the idea that it's *in our weakness* that God is made strong. In one of the oldest texts in all of Scripture, if not the very oldest, God tells His beloved prophet Moses to deliver a series of important reminders to His people. They are framed in the words of a blessing from a loving Father to His daughters and sons:

May the LORD bless you
    and protect you.
May the LORD smile on you
    and be gracious to you.

May the LORD show you his favor
and give you his peace.

NUMBERS 6:24-26

These words are known as the "priestly blessing." In Jewish synagogues and Christian churches all across the world today, they are spoken to worshipers of God because people need to be reminded that God is a God of blessing and protection, of grace and favor and peace. We no longer follow the priestly system, as in Old Testament times, because Jesus serves as our High Priest. But we still desperately need the words of these verses if we hope to shift from feeling heavily burdened to knowing we are richly blessed. Let's look at each reminder in turn.

Blessing #1: God's Presence

The blessing begins, "May the LORD bless you and protect you." Or, as some translations read, "May the LORD bless you and *keep* you" (emphasis added). "To keep" is to save, to hang on to, to preserve, and so what God was asking Moses to remind His followers of was the fact that God is with us. He is here. He is hanging on to us with His "victorious right hand" as Isaiah 41:10 promises (the complete—and completely awesome—text follows).

Don't be afraid, for I am with you.
Don't be discouraged, for I am your God.
I will strengthen you and help you.
I will hold you up with my victorious right hand.

ISAIAH 41:10

It is for this reason that throughout the most tumultuous times, Missy turned to God in prayer. After all, He was already near to her, and He alone held the ultimate power to make things okay. Why *wouldn't* she call out in prayer to Him? Why wouldn't *any* of us ask for His help?

Imagine this rather ridiculous scene: You're washing dishes at the kitchen sink when your young son comes barreling around the corner from the living room, loses his footing on the slippery kitchen floor, and falls flat on his back, right there at your feet. Instead of crying out to you—"Mahhhhhmeeee!"— he just lies there, writhing in pain. He eventually tries to stand up on his own two feet but keeps slipping again and again. You're not trying to be morbid by just standing there—it's more a point of curiosity for you: *Why isn't he choosing to ask for my help? I'm standing right here—can't he see?*

"I'll bless them," God wanted Moses to tell lovers of God. "And I'll *keep* them at every turn."

⤞ WITH YOUR GROUP ⤝

Put words to the rhythms of your prayer life. When do you pray? Where? What do you typically pray for? What is the purpose of prayer, as you understand it? Do you "hear" from God? If so, what is that communication like?

Think back on the journey you've been on, the one that is centered on the impossible burden you've been asked to bear.

On the low days along the way, the days when you slipped and fell again and again, how likely were you to turn to God in prayer and ask for His help to see you through? Log your thoughts on the following lines, completing the sentence you find there.

During my most difficult days, prayer has been . . .

_____

_____

_____

To neglect praying to God is to pass up crucial assistance, even as you are writhing around on the floor. God is near. *He's already here.* And He wants nothing more than to help. "I'll keep them," God wanted Moses to tell God's beloved children. "I'll protect them each step of the way."

How about asking Him to make good on that promise right now?

Spend a few minutes asking God to show you how He has *already* protected you, saved you, upheld you, and kept you along this journey you've been on. Then, on the following lines, jot down the thoughts that come to mind.

_____

_____

_____

_____

_____

_____

_____

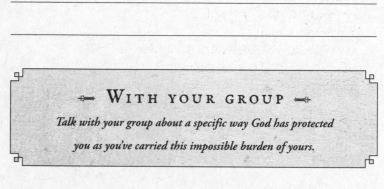

✦ WITH YOUR GROUP ✦

Talk with your group about a specific way God has protected
you as you've carried this impossible burden of yours.

If you've never before made a habit of talking with God in prayer, consider starting now. Bring Him your real questions and your raw feelings about your impossible burden and ask Him to hang on to you as you face the day.

∞

When Jesus ministered here on earth with His disciples, He taught them how to pray using a template known as the Lord's Prayer. That prayer includes a handful of key things God wants us to pray for. On the grid that follows, take a look at the element of prayer noted on the left side, each of which is taken from Matthew 6:9-13. Then, on the right side, write down how you'd put words to that element, according to the burden you carry.

THE LORD'S PRAYER

Our Father in heaven,
    may your name be kept holy.
May your Kingdom come soon.
May your will be done on earth,
    as it is in heaven.
Give us today the food we need,
and forgive us our sins,
    as we have forgiven those who sin against us.
And don't let us yield to temptation,
    but rescue us from the evil one.

MATTHEW 6:9-13

ELEMENT OF PRAYER	WHAT I WOULD PRAY FOR IN LIGHT OF IT
Praise: "Our Father in heaven, may your name be kept holy" (verse 9).	
Perspective: "May your Kingdom come soon" (verse 10).	
Surrender: "May your will be done on earth, as it is in heaven" (verse 10).	
Provision: "Give us today the food we need" (verse 11).	
Forgiveness: "And forgive us our sins, as we have forgiven those who sin against us" (verse 12).	
Protection: "And don't let us yield to temptation, but rescue us from the evil one" (verse 13).	

Which of the elements of prayer from the left-hand column would be most helpful to you today? A heart that yearns to praise God? A deeper resolve to keep a Kingdom perspective in mind? A spirit ready and willing to surrender to God's leadership in your life? Assurance that God really will meet your needs? The reminder that your sins are forgiven and you can be washed clean from their effects as you walk with Christ? Encouragement that you don't have to fumble and fail today, because in Him you have overcome? Make your choice from the following list, and then note beside it the reason for your selection.

☐ Praise: _____

☐ Perspective: _____

☐ Surrender: _____

☐ Provision: _____

☐ Forgiveness: _____

☐ Protection: _____

Now talk with God in prayer about the need that you picked.

As Missy discovered during some of her most difficult days, there is no substitute for candid, consistent conversation with the God who formed us, who loves us, and who is committed to bringing beauty from our pain. Take Him at His Word that He is near to you and longs to help you. Today, practice His presence as you go.

⊷ WITH YOUR GROUP ⊷

*Share with the rest of your group the element of the Lord's
Prayer you are most in need of today. Then, as a group,
spend a few minutes in prayer, telling God of your collective
needs. Consider closing your time of prayer by reciting in
unison the words to the Lord's Prayer, found on page 77.*

Blessing #2: God's Pleasure

The second part of the priestly blessing says, "May the LORD
smile on you and be gracious to you," or in some translations, "make his face to shine upon you" (ESV, NRSV). The
image here is just fantastic. If you have children, then you've
probably had the experience of hoisting a child above you
with your arms extended toward the sky, the child squealing
in waves of giggles about being so far off the ground. The
picture here is one of sheer delight, and it is *this* picture of
joy that God wanted Moses to convey.

Missy experienced this same sensation of her heavenly
Father delighting in her when she received the news that
Mia's orthodontist had perfected a new invention that would
allow Mia to forgo having the halo device screwed into her
skull. The orthodontist had done all the hard work, but
instinctively, Missy knew whom to thank: *God.* "All I could
think of was how grateful I was to my Father in heaven. He
had done this," Missy wrote.

Good parents lavish their children with loving acts for no other reason than that they love them. This is what God was up to in the life of His beloved daughter Missy that day.

Depending on a whole host of variables, including your family of origin, your feelings now toward your father and your husband, and your firsthand experiences throughout life, you probably have a strong reaction—whether positive or negative—to the idea that God delights in you. On the lines that follow, complete the sentence you find there.

God delights in me? This strikes me as . . .

_____

_____

_____

_____

_____

Now, take a look at the following list of adjectives. Which of these words would be true for you if you more fully embraced the idea that, despite the heavy burden God has allowed into your life, He loves you as a proud father loves His child, and that He earnestly and enthusiastically delights in you? Circle all that apply.

Accepted	*Liked*	*Seen*
Admired	*Spurred On*	*Heard*
Affirmed	*Energized*	*Valued*
Encouraged	*Peaceful*	*Accompanied*
Beloved	*Proud*	*Rescued*
Appreciated	*Strong*	*Protected*
Embraced	*Empowered*	*Cared For*
Forgiven	*Victorious*	*Understood*

When a young child knows that her parents delight in her, she tends to exhibit steadiness and peace. She is sure of their presence and love, and she trusts that she is safe. In fact, *all* of those adjectives in the list are true for such a child.

Similarly, when we feel loved and accepted, energized and at peace—when we believe God *delights* in us—we approach all of life, both the cheerful celebrations and the circumstances we wish would go away, with supernatural optimism and strength. This is how we are able to "be brave and keep going," as Missy's family says, not by pulling ourselves up by our bootstraps, but by finding our courage and can't-stop-me grit *in the Lord*.

For Missy, a clear picture of God's delight involved that conversation with Mia's orthodontist. What about you? When have you detected the delight of your heavenly Father, even as you've walked this burdensome path? What was the effect of that experience? Describe the scene in the space that follows, using the prompts to help organize your thoughts.

Looking back, I remember a specific occasion when I sensed the delight of God. It involved . . .

Feeling connected to God in a positive way in that moment was significant to me because . . .

Knowing that God is with me and "for me" helps me remember that . . .

⟀ WITH YOUR GROUP ⟀

Share the "scene" that you wrote about with your group. Why is it such a difference maker for us to focus on God's delight in us?

Despite what the enemy of our souls—Satan—would have us believe, our burdens aren't proof that God is angry with us. Far from it. They are *real manifestations* of living in a *real, fallen world.* Thankfully, God assures us that He will be with us as we face all that fallenness, and His pleasure will rest on our lives. We will look more specifically at how to overcome evidences of fallenness in Blessing #3. But for now, respond to that sentiment. On the following lines, log your thoughts and feelings about this truth.

_____

_____

_____

_____

_____

Blessing #3: God's Provision

The third and final part of the priestly blessing is this: "May the LORD show you his favor and give you his peace" (Numbers 6:26), two divine gifts that are impossible to beat. Perhaps the greatest manifestation of God's "favor" comes by way of the gift of His grace. It has been said that grace is God's **R**iches **A**t **C**hrist's **E**xpense, the idea that because Jesus bore the full weight of our sins on the cross and thus served as the sacrifice God required in order to make right all of our wrongs, we now have full access to God's rich resources. Because Christ died, we forever can live. Grace helps us keep things in perspective because it reminds us that if Christ had not been willing to die, we'd be destitute, despondent, and alone. Every good thing we have comes to us by way of Christ. *All of life is a gift* when you view life through this lens. Before we move on to exploring the gift of peace, take a few moments to answer the following two questions.

1. *What "riches" do you know today because of Christ's sacrifice for you? Freedom from insecurity? Deep and abiding joy? Hope for the future? Something else? Write your response here.*

2. *What attitudes and actions are prompted in you the more you focus on God's great gift of grace? Acts of kindness and compassion? Gratitude? A sense of being at rest? Note your thoughts below.*

⇥ WITH YOUR GROUP ⇤

Discuss with your group members your answer to question #2, mentioning a few of the attitudes and actions you see emerging in yourself the more you focus your attention on God's grace.

Now, to the second gift God articulated at the end of the priestly blessing—peace. Isn't that a beautiful word? Even the mere appearance of it makes our blood pressure drop a few ticks. Say it aloud: *peace*. We are hardwired to love that word.

To round out your understanding of the biblical definition of peace, refer to the Scriptures on pages 85–86, noting the most impactful truth you find in each verse or passage. The first one has been completed for you.

peace   noun | \ʹpes\

1. Romans 8:6 <u>When I let the Holy Spirit control my</u>
<u>thoughts, I will be led to life and peace.</u>

2. John 14:27 _____

_____

3. John 16:33 _____

_____

4. Philippians 4:6-7 _____

_____

5. Isaiah 26:3 _____

_____

⤜ WITH YOUR GROUP ⤛

Which of the biblical truths about peace feels most significant
to you, and why? Discuss your thoughts with your group.

WHAT DOES THE BIBLE SAY
ABOUT PEACE?

→ *Letting your sinful nature control your mind leads to death.*
But letting the Spirit control your mind leads to life and peace.
(Romans 8:6)

→ *I am leaving you with a gift—peace of mind and heart. And*
the peace I give is a gift the world cannot give. So don't be
troubled or afraid. (John 14:27)

→ *I have told you all this so that you may have peace in me. Here on earth you will have many trials and sorrows. But take heart, because I have overcome the world. (John 16:33)*

→ *Don't worry about anything; instead, pray about everything. Tell God what you need, and thank him for all he has done. Then you will experience God's peace, which exceeds anything we can understand. His peace will guard your hearts and minds as you live in Christ Jesus. (Philippians 4:6-7)*

→ *You will keep in perfect peace all who trust in you, all whose thoughts are fixed on you! (Isaiah 26:3)*

The peace of God is a profound gift indeed. It lifts us up, settles us down, provides necessary perspective, and helps us stay the course. During Mia's last "real" meal prior to her distraction surgery, she told Miss Kay that she wasn't nervous about the procedure she'd endure the next day, even as she fully understood how serious that procedure was. Although Mia didn't use the word "peace" in her description of her feelings, Missy knew that peace is exactly what her daughter felt. Mia was not troubled, not afraid, not fretful, not overcome. Her heart and mind were guarded from fear. Her thoughts were not of death, but of life. Sounds a lot like peace, don't you think? Oh, the marvelous gift of peace.

On the following lines, describe what peace looks or feels like to you, even if you've never used that specific word to name it.

Peace . . . as I've known it:

_____

_____

_____

_____

_____

The solution to every problem this fallen world throws at us is found in looking at that problem through the lenses of grace and peace. This is why God was so adamant that Moses should conclude the blessings this way. He knew that each time we struggled, each time we picked up another burden to bear, we'd be tempted to forget that He has already given us every good thing we need to live lives of satisfaction, victory, and joy. And so we keep our supernatural spectacles on, choosing to focus not on the obstacles and challenges, but rather on God's perfect gifts of *grace* and *peace*. In Christ, we have access to God's riches. And in our inner person, we are at rest.

What's more, the grace and peace we enjoy in Christ aren't intended for our enjoyment alone. Perhaps the most gratifying part of this whole deal is that once we embrace this approach to life, we get to turn around and bless others too. This is where things get good.

Blessed to Be a Blessing

It has been said that you can't give what you don't have—and certainly, this is true. But the opposite is also true: What you have, you can give away. And as it relates to bearing impossible burdens, we have a powerful message to proclaim: God is near to the brokenhearted. God has granted us grace and peace. God promises to provide for our needs. God says He never will leave us alone.

Imagine for a moment the influence you could have if you took these themes to your circle of friends. As a first step, on the following grid note the impossible burdens you're aware of that are being carried by your loved ones.

LOVED ONE	THE BURDEN BEING CARRIED

Next, select just one person's name from the grid, and on the lines that follow, log your ideas for how the promise of God's nearness, the promise of His pleasure, or the promise of His grace and peace might be helpful to that family member or friend.

_____

_____

_____

As Missy describes in the final chapter of her book, she has seen this ripple effect of blessings play out firsthand. God has given her family incredible opportunities to minister to others who are impacted by cleft palates and cleft lips, and because she, Jase, and Mia have chosen to rest in the capable arms of their loving Father instead of growing bitter or angry about their plight, they have had the experience, energy, and enthusiasm to be conduits of optimism and hope. They understand that they are blessed to be a blessing. The same is true for us.

We Are Blessed . . .

As you trust that God is at work behind the scenes of your impossible burden—bringing beauty from ashes, bringing dancing from sorrow, and bringing peace from deepest pain—you receive His blessing as truth. In your heart and soul, you personalize the promises that God delivered through Moses all those centuries ago. Read aloud the following personalized version of that Numbers 6 account:

> _The Lord blesses me and protects me._
> _The Lord smiles on me and is gracious to me._
> _The Lord shows me His favor_
> _and always, always gives me His peace._
> _Amen and amen._

You are blessed. Can you see it now? Despite your heavy burden, you are *blessed*. And it's not for your life's enrichment only, as we've discussed. You are blessed so that you can pass blessing on.

. . . *To Be a Blessing*

As you engage with the people around you, many of whom are surely as heavily burdened as you've been, you can look them in the eye and say with confidence, "I know you're hurting, but God is here to help."

By your words and by your actions, you can bless them as you have been blessed. "The Lord longs to bless you and protect you," you can say. "The Lord is smiling on you and is gracious toward you. The Lord will show you His favor and give you His peace, if only you'll devote yourself to Him."

Behind every burden is a blessing. All that's left is for us to receive.

⊶ WITH YOUR GROUP ⊷

In the same way that generations of Christ followers have taken courage from the victorious stories of Moses, Job, the apostle Paul, and Jesus Christ, what do you make of the idea that your loved ones could actually be blessed by the manner in which you respond to the burdens you bear?

Notes, Resolutions, Ponderings, and Such

Parting Thoughts from Missy
BE BRAVE AND KEEP GOING

In recent years, the mantra that has encircled our family and inspired us to persevere when things felt hard is this: "Be brave and keep going." I wish I could take credit for coming up with that phrase, but I cannot. While shopping in the quaint town of Ruidoso, New Mexico, Mia and her cousin Merritt found necklaces[6] touting those inspiring words. Immediately, I bought three of them—one for each of the girls and one for me—and I told Mia that we could wear them in support of her upcoming surgery. She liked that idea, and she and Merritt put them on that day.

The phrase jumped out at me because it summed up

perfectly the two characteristics we would all need to manifest in the coming days: courage and good old-fashioned doggedness. I was keenly aware of what my daughter was about to go through—yet another time. I knew that not only was she going to have to be brave when it came to preoperative appointments and the surgery itself, but that she was going to have to keep up that courageous spirit while enduring an arduous recovery. Twelve weeks it was going to take in order for healing to have its way.

How many times have we prayed for someone who has lost a family member to an unexpected death, a close friend who just found out he has cancer, or a church member who is walking through a divorce that she never expected to face? While all of these incidents require a tremendous amount of bravery, these circumstances are never quickly overcome. It's easy for us to forget to keep praying and encouraging after the funeral is over, the surgery is complete, and the divorce has been finalized. But so many times, the hardest part is just beginning. Life's big-deal difficulties require weeks, months, even years of fearlessness and steadfastness before we sense that any progress is being made.

I decided to put the phrase on a necklace and sell it to raise money for the Mia Moo Fund, a nonprofit organization started in 2014 that provides awareness, support, and funding for families impacted by cleft lip and palate. To my surprise, we raised thousands of dollars in just a few days. What's more, hundreds of people who bought the necklace posted comments on social media sites about how they, too, had faced or were facing a challenging situation in life, and that they desperately needed the gentle reminder that their circumstances didn't have to capsize them. They really could muster ongoing courage—to rise up, meet their challenge head-on, and prevail in the end. They really could "be brave and keep going."

The truth is, we all can.

To download your "Be Brave and Keep Going" printable, visit www.BlessedBlessedBlessed.com,

and follow the movement on Twitter #blessedblessedblessed.

Postscript:
Good News for Everyone

⁓

How I hope the experience you've just worked through has proven useful, encouraging, and practical as you devote yourself to finding the blessing hiding behind your "impossible burden." Believe me, Jase and I know how heavy those burdens can be. Which is why it has been a profound relief in our lives to know that God gladly bears our burdens, as He promises in Matthew 11:28-30. We looked at these verses earlier, but perhaps now the words will have greater reach in your mind and heart: "Come to me," Jesus said, "all of you who are weary and carry heavy burdens, and I will give you rest. Take my yoke upon you. Let me teach you, because I am humble and gentle at heart, and you will find rest for your souls. For my yoke is easy to bear, and the burden I give you is light."

If I were to sum up what it means to be a Christian, or to walk with Christ, or to be born again, I would point to that passage, for starters. A person who loves God and is committed to living like Christ is first and foremost someone who *is open to Christ's teaching.* This person isn't living according to his or her own ways and whims but instead looks to the example of Jesus—and to the infallible Word of God, the Bible—for direction in decisions and steps.

There, in God's Word, we discover that all people sin, according to Romans 3:23, but that we sinners can be redeemed by trusting in Jesus Christ (Romans 3:24). This is really, really good news because *all* of us are responsible for the death Jesus endured. Sin is a *human* condition, and it was our sin that separated us from God. The idea that our relationship with Him can be restored is a beautiful and powerful theme that all of Scripture points to, and it was this theme I began to internalize when I was just a teenager, just starting the process of sorting out this thing called life.

After Jesus was crucified, declared dead, and buried in a tomb, God raised Him from the dead and had Him return to His disciples, who were understandably floored by this turn of events. Weeks later, He ascended back into heaven to take His rightful position at the right hand of His Father, and it was after that that the Holy Spirit came upon the believers who were gathered together (Acts 1–2). One of Jesus' apostles, Peter, preached a rousing sermon to a crowd that was cut to the heart by what they heard, and ever since that day, believers gather together week after week to proclaim the news that Jesus is alive, that His Spirit is ready to guide people in truth, and that the abundant life we are desperate for is actually available here and now.

We access these great gifts simply by choosing to *believe.*

The Bible says that whoever confesses Christ with his or her mouth and chooses to believe in His name (see Romans 10:9) will live eternally with God. It also is clear that whoever refuses to obey the gospel of Christ will live forever separated from Him (2 Thessalonians 1:8).

I may not have known a lot about the ins and outs of life at age thirteen, but one thing I was clear on is that I did *not* want to be separated from God. And so one night when Jase and I were sharing the message of Christ with a married couple, as we had done hundreds of times before, I turned to Jase and said, "I need to do what I'm asking them to do." I had known the facts for years, but I had never really let Christ "in." Like those people gathered before Peter as he preached that day, I was cut to the heart by the truth of God's Word, and I knew I needed to surrender my life to God and be "born again."

∽

The book of John tells the story of a man named Nicodemus, a religious leader who, like me, had all the facts about Jesus but didn't have a personal relationship with Him. As the story goes, one night Nicodemus approached Jesus to ask Him about what following Him would entail. Jesus cut right to the chase: "I tell you the truth, unless you are born again, you cannot see the Kingdom of God" (John 3:3). To Nicodemus, this sounded ridiculous. How could a full-grown man be born again?

Jesus, ever patient and ever loving, looked at Nicodemus and said, "Humans can reproduce only human life, but the Holy Spirit gives birth to spiritual life. So don't be surprised when I say, 'You must be born again'" (John 3:6-7).

We are so much like Nicodemus, aren't we? We focus so much on "human life" that we forget there is another realm at work all around us, and also, for those of us who have the Holy Spirit *within* us—it's the *spiritual life* about which Jesus spoke.

The night I realized that despite all of my head knowledge about spiritual matters, I'd never actually been born again, Jase immediately drove me to our church, and he baptized me on the spot into Jesus's death, burial, and resurrection, as Romans 6:1-4 talks about. Finally. Based on my confession of Christ as Lord, I was gloriously born again. That night, I "put on Christ" as Galatians 3:27 so beautifully says.

It was the process of walking with Christ and learning from Him that I began that night that sustained me years later, during some of my soul's darkest, bleakest nights. It was the wisdom of the Lord that anchored me when the seas around me raged. It was the wisdom of the Lord that strengthened me when I thought I couldn't take another step. It was the wisdom of the Lord that reminded me that Mia's struggles weren't caused by something I'd done or neglected to do. There's a story in John 9 about a man who had been born blind. Jesus' disciples approached Him and asked, "Why was this man born blind? Was it because of his own sins or his parents' sins?" (verses 1-2). Jesus' answer still causes me to come undone. "It was not because of his sins or his parents' sins," Jesus said. "This happened so the power of God could be seen in him" (verse 3).

The good news for me was that, even in spite of my family's intense struggle, God's power could be revealed. But an even bigger "aha" from this story is that *regardless of the situation in which we find ourselves—whether of our own making or otherwise—God's power can be revealed.* He is in the business of making beauty from ashes, which is something I consistently need to be told.

Whatever burdens we carry, they won't last forever. Earthly burdens never do. What's more, 2 Corinthians 4:17 promises that the present troubles we're dealing with will actually "produce for us a glory that vastly outweighs them and will last forever!" Eternal glory that outweighs temporal grief? I'll take it! How about you?

The text goes on to say that it is for this reason we choose not to look at the troubles we can see but rather "fix our gaze on things that cannot be seen" (2 Corinthians 4:18). What it's talking about here is *Christ*, our unseen but incomparable companion along this somewhat bumpy journey called life.

I hope you'll decide to join me and the millions of others who are committing themselves to the way of Jesus, day by day, hour by hour, breath by sometimes-labored breath. Come along as we follow Jesus, the One who exchanges blessings for the burdens we lay at His feet. And when you do, please let me know by tweeting me at #blessedblessedblessed.

Notes

❧

1. John 16:33
2. 2 Corinthians 12:9
3. 1 Corinthians 13:12
4. Kevin Clark, "Andrew Luck: The NFL's Most Perplexing Trash Talker," *Wall Street Journal*, December 16, 2014, http://www.wsj.com/articles /andrew-luck-the-nfls-most-perplexing-trash-talker-1418663249.
5. Numbers 6:24-26
6. While the original necklace that Mia and Merritt found was much different than the one Missy redesigned with the phrase, it certainly inspired her creation. To order one for yourself or a loved one, visit www.missyrobertson.com. Added bonus: All proceeds support the Mia Moo Fund.

About the Authors

~

Missy Robertson stars in the record-breaking reality television series A&E's *Duck Dynasty*. She is a devoted mother, a sought-after public speaker, and the creator of her own clothing line. She participates in mission work in the United States and internationally, including serving with an orphanage in the Dominican Republic. She is cofounder of the Mia Moo Fund, an organization dedicated to raising awareness and funds to help domestic children and their families affected by cleft lip and palate. Missy and Jase have been married for twenty-five years and live in West Monroe, Louisiana, with their three children: Reed, Cole, and Mia.

Ashley Wiersma is a freelance writer and video producer of Christian living, leadership, and spiritual memoir products. She lives with her husband and daughter in Monument, Colorado.

MIA MOO

because every kid deserves a smile

THE MIA MOO FUND is a nonprofit organization created by Jase, Missy, and Mia Robertson. The Mia Moo Fund is dedicated to raising awareness and funds toward the management, treatments, and surgical procedures for domestic children affected by cleft lip and palate. We at the Mia Moo Fund want to inform and inspire families and improve the quality of life for children born with cleft lip and palate. Our overall desire is that these children learn that they have a wonderful and unique purpose in life that only they can fulfill.

To learn more and donate, please visit MiaMoo.org.